Sophocles'
Antigone
In Plain and Simple English

BookCaps™ Study Guides
www.bookcaps.com

© 2012. All Rights Reserved.

Table of Contents

Characters

ANTIGONE and **ISMENE** - daughters of Oedipus and sisters of Polyneices

and Eteocles.

CREON, King of Thebes.

HAEMON, Son of Creon, betrothed to Antigone.

EURYDICE, wife of Creon.

TEIRESIAS, the prophet.

CHORUS, of Theban elders.

A WATCHMAN

A MESSENGER

A SECOND MESSENGER

ANTIGONE and **ISMENE** before the Palace gates.

Argument

Antigone, daughter of Oedipus, the dead King of Thebes, resolves to bury her brother Polyneices, killed in his attack on Thebes. This defies the order of Creon, who now rules Thebes. She is caught in the act and brought before the king. She justifies her action by saying that she must follow the laws of Heaven despite what any man might say. Creon, unmoved, orders that she should be walled up in a cave. His son Haemon, Antigone's fiancé, pleads in vain for her life and threatens to die with her. Warned by the prophet Teiresias Creon repents and rushes to release Antigone. But he is too late: he finds Antigone dead from suicide and Haemon kills himself in front of Creon. Returning to the palace he sees within the dead body of his queen, who stabbed herself through the heart when she heard of her son's death.

ANTIGONE

Ismene, sister of my blood and heart,
Do you see how Zeus wants to make us suffer
The curse of Oedipus, a world of sorrow!
For what pain, affliction, outrage, shame,
Is missing from our fortunes, yours and mine?
And now today's proclamation,
Made by our leader to the State,
What is its purpose? Did you hear and note it,
Or are you deaf when friends are exiled as enemies?

ISMENE

To me, Antigone, I haven't had any word of friends,
Good or bad, since we two
Were stripped of our two brothers in one day
When they killed each other; and since the night
The besiegers from Argos fled, I have had
No further news, saddening or cheering.

ANTIGONE

I knew this was the case, and so I called you
Outside the gates to whisper it to you.

ISMENE

What is it? You have some dark secret.

ANTIGONE

What could it be but the thought of our two dead
brothers,
One given a proper funeral by Creon,
The other denied one? Eteocles
Was put in the ground (so it's said)
With all the customary fitting ceremonies,
So that he would go properly to the underworld.
But Polynieces, a dishonored corpse
Cannot be buried, no-one can grieve for him
(This is what I hear the royal order is);
He must be left without a tomb, without mourners,
A feast for the kites to smell from far off and swoop
upon.
This is the ruling (if the reports are true)
Of Creon, our most noble Creon, aimed
At you and me, yes, me as well; and shortly
He'll be here to spread, for those
Who haven't heard it, his orders;
It's obviously not something
He's taking lightly, as the order says
That anyone who disobeys will be stoned to death.
That's the situation; now it's up to you to show
If you live up to your heritage or not.

ISMENE

But how, my hasty, dear sister, in this case,
Can I do anything, good or bad?

ANTIGONE

Tell me if you'll help and support me. Decide.

6

ISMENE

In what daring venture? What are you thinking of?

ANTIGONE

Help me carry off the corpse.

ISMENE

What, bury him in spite of the order?

ANTIGONE

My brother, and though you won't recognize him
yours too.
No man shall say that I betrayed a brother.

ISMENE

Will you go through with this, though Creon forbids
it?

ANTIGONE

What right has he to keep me from my own family?

ISMENE

Think, sister, what happened to our father,
Hated, dishonored, convicted of sin by himself,
Blinded , his own executioner.

Think of his mother-wife (names which should not go
together),
Killed with a noose she knotted herself,
And lastly, our unlucky brothers, who on the same
day,
Caught up in a shared fate,
Killed themselves, each one killer and victim.
Think, sister, we are left alone;
Will we not die the most wretched death of all,
If against the law we ignore
A monarch's orders? – we are weak women,
remember,
Not built by nature to fight with men.
Remember this too, that the stonger one rules;
We must obey his orders, these or even worse ones.
So I say that I am forced not to do this and ask
The dead to forgive me. I have to obey
The ruling powers. It's stupidity, I think,
To try and rebel against the king in anything.

ANTIGONE

I won't try to persuade you; in fact, if you now said
you would,
I wouldn't want you with me.
Go your own way, I shall bury him alone.
How sweet to die doing such a task, to rest –
A brother and sister linked in a loving hug –
A sinless sinner, condemned a while on earth
But applauded by the dead; and I shall live
With them forever. As for you,
Reject the eternal laws of Heaven if you want.

—

ISMENE

I do not reject them, but I haven't the skill
To stand up to the State or break her laws.

ANTIGONE

A poor excuse. I will go alone
To place my dearest brother in his grave.

ISMENE

My poor, dear sister, how I fear for you!

ANTIGONE

Don't be frightened for me; have a look at yourself.

ISMENE

At least don't tell anyone what you're up to,
Keep it secret and hidden, as I will.

ANTIGONE

Oh, tell everyone, sister; I'll hate you more
If you don't tell the whole town.

ISMENE

You have a brave soul for such dangerous work.

ANTIGONE

I give pleasure to those I would most like to please.

ISMENE

If you succeed; but you're doomed to fail.

ANTIGONE

If my strength fails then so will I, but not before that.

ISMENE

But why try it, when the thing's impossible?

ANTIGONE

Sister, give up, or I shall soon hate you,
And the dead man shall hate you too, justifiably.
Call me mad and leave my madness free
To destroy itself; the worst that can happen
Is that I'll die an honorable death.

ISMENE

[Exeunt]

Have it your own way; it's a mad plan,
But those who love you love you just as much.

CHORUS

(Str. 1)

———

Sunbeam, you are the brightest that ever
Dawned on our seven gated Thebes,
Oh golden eye of day,
How lovely your light shone over Dirce's fountain,
Sending on their hurtling homeward way,
Far quicker than they came, the army of Argos;
Putting to flight the silver shields,
The army with their white decorations.
Against our land the proud invader came
To pursue evil Polyneice's claim,
Like an eagle swooping down
With his snow-white claws.
With a clanging din and a horsetail plume in his
helmet,
The hopeful lord of Argos pressed onwards.

(Ant.1)

He waited, besieging our city walls,
His hungry spearmen at our seven gates,
But before a torch could burn our towers,
Before they'd tasted our blood, they turned,
Forced by the Dragon; in their rear
They heard with panic the noise of war.
For Zeus, who hates arrogance,
Saw that gold covered army;
And as they raised a shout of triumph at reaching
their goal
He struck them with his forked lightning.

(Str. 2)

He smashed down upon the earth,
The firebrand was snatched from the blasphemous
hand,
As he staggered on like a drunk at an orgy,
Breathing hate and flame,
And fell. Elsewhere in the battle
Here, there, great Mars wheeled like a war horse,
Spearing out from his chariot,
And our enemies bit the dust.
Seven captains hammered on
Our seven gates; there was an opponent for each,
And each left behind his bright armor,
A trophy for Zeus who turned the tide;
There were just two who remain, that unfortunate
pair,
Born of the same parents,
Who charged with their lances, one against the other,
Drove them home and both died, brother killed by
brother.

(Ant. 2)

[Enter **CREON**]

Now Victory comes back to Thebes,
And smiles on her plain, circled with chariots.
Now let feast and festival
Blot out the memories of war.
Let us all go to the temples
And dance and sing the whole night through.
god of Thebes, lead the song,
Bacchus, the ground shaker!

———

Now let's stop our celebrations;
Look! Creon, our new lord, is coming,
Crowned, by the twists of fate, our king.
What, I wonder, is he thinking of?
Why has he summoned us? Why has he called
All of the elders,
Calling us to debate with him
Some important affairs of State?

CREON

Elders, the gods have steadied
Our storm-tossed ship of state, now safely in port.
But I have gathered you by special summons
As my most trusted advisers; firstly, because
I know that you were loyal to Laius in the old days,
And then as you were also loyal to Oedipus when he
saved our state,
Both when he ruled and when his rule was finished,
You stayed loyal to the royal family.
Now that his two sons have died in one day,
Brother murdered by brother,
I claim and hold the throne and kingship,
By right of my relation to the dead princes.
But it isn't easy to tell
The strength of a man, of his mind and willpower,
Until it is tested once he's in power;
And for me, if anyone who has the highest power
Dodges following the best policy, not speaking
For fear of the consequences, I have always
Thought that man the lowest of the low.
And I despise the man who puts his friend
Before his country. For myself,

I swear by Zeus, who sees all,
That if I uncover some cunning plan
To damage the State, I will not be silent;
Nor would I have a public enemy
As a private friend, knowing that the State
Is the good ship that carries all our futures:
Friendship will be ended if she is wrecked.
This is my policy as I try
To serve the people, and so
I have issued an order in relation
To the sons of Oedipus: Eteocles,
Who fought and died for his country
As a hero – he should be buried
With all the respect and ceremony
That are the right of the honored dead.
But for that wretched exile who returned,
Meaning with flames to destroy
His father's city and his father's gods,
And satisfy his thirst for revenge with the blood of his
kinsmen,
Or to drag them as prisoners behind his chariot –
For Polynieces I rule that nobody
Shall give him a burial or mourn for him,
But that his corpse should be left unburied as meat
For the dogs and carrion crows, a horrid sight.
This is my decision; never will I let
Scoundrels be honored over true men,
But all good patriots, alive or dead,
Shall be promoted and honored by me.

CHORUS

Son of Menoeceus, that's your choice of how you deal
With the one who loved and the one who loathed our State.
Your word is law; you can do with us,
The living, as you wish, just as you can with the dead.

CREON

Then see you do as I have ordered.

CHORUS

This task should be given to younger men.

CREON

Don't worry, I have sent guards to watch the corpse.

CHORUS

What else do you want us to do?

CREON

Not to allow disobedience.

CHORUS

No man would be so stupid as to risk his death.

CREON

[Enter GUARD]

The penalty is death, but the hope of profit
Has often led men to their downfall.

GUARD

My lord, I will not pretend to puff and pant
As if I'd just run all the way here.
Truly, my soul, under its burden of thoughts,
Often stopped, turned back, turned round again;
My conscience drove me on and pulled me back in turn.
"Why are you rushing headlong to your fate, poor fool?"
She whispered. The she said, "If Creon learns
About this from someone else, it'll be even worse for you."
So I went along my way, sometimes quick, sometimes slow;
Thinking makes short distances long ones.
But in the end the voice saying go forward won,
So I came to face you. I will speak even if I say nothing,
For taking courage in my despair I thought,
"Let the worst happen, all you can do is face your fate."

CREON

What's the news? Why this despair?

GUARD

Can I say a word about my position?
I didn't do the deed or see it done,
And it wouldn't be fair for me to be punished.

CREON

You're a good swordsman, you can fence around
What is obviously an important matter.

GUARD

The bearer of bad news should be afraid.

CREON

Then, sir, say your piece and go.

GUARD

Well, it has to be said; the corpse is buried. Someone
Just now covered it with the dry earth,
Performed the proper ceremony and was gone.

CREON

What are you saying? Who dared to do this?

GUARD

I can't tell, for there were no marks
Of a pickaxe or hoe – hard unbroken ground,
Without a scratch or rut from chariot wheels,

No sign that human hands had been at work.
When the first sentry of the morning shift
Gave the alarm, we were all terrified.
The corpse had vanished, not buried in the earth
But covered with dust, as if someone was trying
To ward off the curse that falls on the unburied dead;
There was no sign of dogs or hungry jackals.
Then a great argument started;
Guards shouted at each other and it seemed a fight
would follow,
For there was no-one to act as peacemaker;
Each one of us was suspected, but nobody could be
proved guilty,
For there was no evidence. We challenged each one
To be tortured, or handle red hot iron,
Or walk through the fire, swearing our innocence
On oath – we neither did this thing
Ourselves, nor did we know who did or planned it.
Our investigation ground to a halt, when one spoke
Who made us all bow down like quivering reeds,
For there was no denying what he said nor any way
To escape his sentence: "You must tell
The King, you cannot hide it." That's what he said,
And he convinced us he was right; we drew lots,
And I, unlucky victim, drew the short straw.
So here I am, unwilling and also
Unwelcome, as no man wants to hear bad news.

CHORUS

I thought from the start, your highness,
That there was something more than natural going on.

18

CREON

Oh be quiet, your babbling annoys me;
It looks like you're going soft in your old age.
Don't you think it's ridiculous to suppose
The gods would care anything for this dead man?
Did they show him special favors,
And bury him like a good man,
The man who came to burn their holy sanctuaries,
To destroy their shrines, lay waste to their land
And break their laws? Or perhaps
The gods like to favor the bad?
No! No! I have noticed for a long time some rebels
Who shook their heads and defied authority,
Disliking my orders and my rule.
It's they, I'll bet, who won over my guards
With bribes. Of all the evils on earth
The worst is money. It's money that sacks
Cities, and drives men out of hearth and home;
It twists and perverts natural innocence,
And encourages dishonesty.
But those who sold themselves will find their greed
Has got the better of them, and they'll regret it sooner
or later.
Yes, as I still respect the rule of Zeus,
I swear by Zeus, that unless you find and bring
Into my presence the very man
Who performed this lawless burial,
Then death will not be punishment enough for you.
You will be hanged on a cross, and while still alive
You will confess to this outrage. That will teach you
And give you what you deserve.
There are some crimes that bring no profit.

Only a few do well through dishonesty,
Most come to ruin and disgrace.

GUARD

May I say something, or must I turn and go
Without a word?

CREON

Go! Can't you see
Even the question irritates me?

GUARD

Where, my lord?
Does it irritate your ears, or your heart?

CREON

Why should I want to find exactly where it hurts?

GUARD

I irritate your ears, but whoever did this irritates your
mind.

CREON

What a load of drivel! Get out!

GUARD

Driveling perhaps, but innocent.

CREON

You're doubly guilty, having sold your soul for gain.

GUARD

Alas! How sad when clever men think wrongly.

CREON

[Exit **CREON**]

Go, and stop this rubbish. If you fail
To find the criminals, you will find
The price of ill-gotten gains is death.

GUARD

I pray he may be found. But caught or not
(And that's down to fate) you shall never
See me coming back here, that's for sure.
For I have escaped, which is more than I thought or
hoped for,
And for my safety I owe much thanks to the gods.

CHORUS

(Str. 1)

There are many wonderful things,
But none more wonderful than man;

Over the surging sea,
With the south wind blowing,
Through the waves of the bay,
Man makes his dangerous journey;
And on the oldest of gods, Earth,
That knows no strain or decay,
He always scratches and digs,
With his horses yoked together
As a team,
Turning round the plough.

(Ant. 1)

The empty headed birds of the air,
The beasts of the fields and woods,
He can catch with his woven nets,
And the same for the fish in the waters.
He is the master of cunning:
The savage bull, and the deer
Who roam free on the mountains,
Are tamed by his ultimate skill;
And the shaggy rough maned horse
Is broken to obey the reins.

(Str. 2)

Speech, and the speed
Of wisdom and laws,
He has learnt all these for himself;
And the arrowing rain that flies
And the freezing air
Beneath the open winter sky,
He can deal with them all:

———

He has learned to cope with terrible illness,
He can cope with anything,
But he hasn't found a cure for death.

(Ant. 2)

[Enter **GUARD** bringing **ANTIGONE**]

Greater than the fastest flight though
Is the cunning and skill
That sometimes leads man to the light
But sometimes towards evil.
If he follows the law
And respects the gods of the State
His city shall stand proud;
But a cityless exile is the man
Who from his pride
Leaves the path of righteousness.
I hope I never sit next to him.
Or know what goes on in his heart.
What's this strange sight I see,
Which fills me with astonishment?
Sure, I know her, it's her,
The maid Antigone,
Unfortunate child of an unfortunate father,
Did you recklessly plot,
Madly go against the King's orders?
Is that why they're dragging you?

GUARD

Here is the culprit, caught in the act
Of giving burial. But where's the King?

CHORUS

[Enter **CREON**]

There he is, coming back from the palace just in time.

CREON

Just in time for what? What has happened?

GUARD

No man, my lord, should make a vow, for if
He swears he won't do something
You can be sure he'll change his mind afterwards.
When I ran from the hailstorm of your threats
I swore that you would not see me here again;
But the excitement of a bit of good luck
Is intoxicating, so I'm here against my vow.
And here's my prisoner, caught in the act,
Decorating the grave. No drawing lots this time,
This prize is mine by right of finding.
So, take her, judge her, torture her, if you will.
She's yours, my king, but I can justly claim
That I can leave here without a stain on my character.

CREON

Tell me how you arrested the girl, and where.

GUARD

Burying the man. That's all that needs saying.

CREON

Have you gone mad? Do you know what you're
saying?

GUARD

I saw this woman burying the corpse
Against your orders. Is that plain enough?

CREON

But how was she caught in the act?

GUARD

This is how it happened. No sooner had we got there,
Driven away from you by your awful threats,
Than we at once swept away all traces of dust
And uncovered the slimy body. Then we sat
High on the ridge upwind of the stench,
While each man kept his mate awake and loudly
Abused the slacker if he happened to drop off.
So we watched all night, until the sun
Was high in the sky, with his blazing beams
Beating down on us. A sudden whirlwind then
whipped up
A cloud of dust that blotted out the sky,
Swept across the plain, tore the leaves from the trees,
And shook the sky. We closed our eyes
And waited for this assault from heaven to finish.

At last it did and lo! there stood this girl.
She gave a piercing cry, sad and shrill,
Like a mother bird which sees its nest
Robbed of its chicks; this was how the girl
Wailed as she saw the body stripped and bare,
And she cursed the ruffians who had done it.
Soon she gathered handfuls of dry dust,
Then, holding up a well made bronze jug,
She poured three streams of water on the dead man.
At the sight we leapt on her and grabbed
Our prey. She stood unworried, and when
We accused her of the previous crime and this
She denied nothing. I was happy – and sad;
It's sweet to escape punishment oneself,
But to bring disaster on a friend
Is bad. But all in all, I think
A man's first duty is to look after himself.

CREON

Speak, girl, with your head bent low and downcast
eyes,
Do you plead guilty or deny it?

ANTIGONE

Guilty, I don't deny it.

CREON (to GUARD)

(To ANTIGONE)

Sir, go where you want, and thank

Your lucky stars that you've escaped a serious charge.

(To **ANTIGONE**)

Now, answer this simple question, yes or no;
Did you know about the order?

ANTIGONE

I knew, I knew everything; how could I not know?

CREON

And yet you were bold enough to break the law?

ANTIGONE

Yes, for these are not the laws of Zeus,
And Justice, who sits on her throne at his feet,
Did not make these human laws.
Nor did I consider that you, a mortal man,
Could as you chose cancel and overrule
The unchangeable unwritten laws of Heaven.
They were not made today or yesterday;
They never die, and nobody knows where they come from.
I do not fear the displeasure of any mortal man, so I wasn't going
To disobey these laws and so provoke
Heaven's anger. I knew I must die sometime,
Even if you hadn't ordered it; if by this death
Comes quicker, that will please me.

For death is a pleasure to one whose life, like mine,
Is full of sorrow. So my situation seems
Not sad, but full of joy; if I had tolerated
Leaving my mother's son there unburied
I would have a reason to be sad, but now I have not.
And if you say this makes me a fool,
I say that proves you're a fool yourself.

CHORUS

A stubborn daughter of a stubborn father,
This unfortunate girl tries to hit back at her punisher.

CREON

Well, she will learn that the most stubborn wills
Are the easiest to bend, just as the hardest iron,
Overheated in the fire until it's brittle,
Is the one that is quickest to break into fragments
when it's beaten.
A bit calms the liveliest horse, and he
Who is under another's power must be humble.
But this proud girl, well taught in insolence,
First broke the law of the land, and then –
A second and more insolent act –
Boasts and celebrates her wickedness.
Now if she was allowed to do these things
Unpunished, I'm the woman and she the man.
But though she is my sister's child, and closer
Family than any of my household,
Neither she nor her sister will escape
The ultimate penalty, for I judge that they are both,

As co-conspirators, equally guilty.
Bring out the older one; just now I saw her
Inside the palace, wild and upset.
The workings of the mind often show
The dark secret deeds, before they are done.
More horrible still is the criminal who tries,
When caught, to make a virtue of the crime.

ANTIGONE

Are you going to do more than kill your prisoner?

CREON

No, your life is mine and that's enough.

ANTIGONE

Why are you waiting then? There's no word of yours
That is pleasant to me; god forbid it ever would be,
And you hate me just as much.
But how else could I have got such a great reputation,
If it wasn't for this act of burying my brother?
That's what all the townspeople would say,
If they weren't gagged by terror.
A king has many privileges, and one of the greatest
Is that all his acts and all his words are law.

CREON

You're the only one in Thebes who thinks like this.

ANTIGONE

They all think like me, but hold their tongues around you.

CREON

You don't think your shame makes you different to them?

ANTIGONE

To respect one's family is not shameful.

CREON

Wasn't his dead enemy your family too?

ANTIGONE

One mother carried them and they had the same father.

CREON

So why insult one by honoring the other?

ANTIGONE

The dead man would not think like you.

CREON

I'm sure you're right, if good and evil still exist.

ANTIGONE

That dead man was no villain but my brother.

CREON

The patriot was killed with the outlaw's weapon.

ANTIGONE

Whatever, the underworld requires these ceremonies.

CREON

They don't require that scum should be treated the same as the brave.

ANTIGONE

Who knows, maybe crimes in this world are good deeds there.

CREON

Not even death can make an enemy a friend.

ANTIGONE

I lean towards love, not hatred.

CREON

[Enter **ISMENE**]

Die then, and love the dead if you want;
No woman shall be master whilst I'm alive.

CHORUS

Look, from the doors of the palace,
Here comes Isemene, weeping
For her sister's fate; see her brow,
Once so serene, now frowning,
And her lovely face is covered
With an angry red flush.

CREON

The woman who, like an unseen viper,
Hid in my house and drained my blood.
It seems I nourished two curses
To attack my throne. Tell me, did you help
In this crime, or do you deny all knowledge?

ISMENE

I did the deed, if she says so,
And I will share the guilt with my sister.

ANTIGONE

That would not be fair. You wouldn't help me
At first, and I rejected your partnership.

ISMENE

But now you are caught, I feel strengthened
To claim an equal share of punishment.

ANTIGONE

Who did this the underworld knows;
Someone who's friendly in words not deeds is no
friend of mine.

ISMENE

Oh sister, do not reject me, but let me share
Your good deed, and die with you.

ANTIGONE

Don't claim a deed you weren't involved in;
One death is enough. Why should you die?

ISMENE

What could life offer me if you're gone?

ANTIGONE

Ask Creon, he's your family and best friend.

ISMENE

Why do you taunt me? Do you enjoy causing me
pain?

ANTIGONE

It's a sad joke, if indeed I'm joking.

ISMENE

Say if there's any help I can give, even now.

ANTIGONE

No, save yourself; I don't begrudge you escaping.

ISMENE

Will you refuse even this favor, that I should share your fate?

ANTIGONE

Yes, for you chose life and I chose death.

ISMENE

You can't say I didn't tell you not to.

ANTIGONE

Well, some agreed with you, some with me.

ISMENE

But now we are both convicted, just the same.

ANTIGONE

Do not fear; you live, I died long before
I gave my life to save the dead.

CREON

Both girls, I think, are mad. One has just
Lost her mind, the other was born mad.

ISMENE

Yes my lord, when misfortune comes
Even the wisest can lose their minds.

CREON

You lost your mind when you decided
To become a criminal.

ISMENE

What life is there for me if I don't have my sister?

CREON

Don't talk as if your sister's here; she's dead.

ISMENE

What, will you kill your son's fiancée?

CREON

Yes, he can plough a different field.

ISMENE

No new engagement could match the first one.

CREON

Curse these sluts who chase and seduce our sons.

ANTIGONE

Oh Haemon, how your father insults you!

CREON

A curse on you and your damned bride!

CHORUS

What, will you take your son's bride from him?

CREON

It's death that will stop this marriage, not his father.

CHORUS

So her death warrant is sealed, it seems.

CREON

By you, as it was first by me. Take them away, guards,
And keep a close eye on them. From now on let them learn
To live as women should, not wandering about the world.
Even the bravest might try to run
When they see death snapping at their heels.

CHORUS

(Str. 1)

The ones who have never known pain are triply blessed!
If the curse of heaven lands once on a family,
The stain stays and quickly spreads,
Age after age, so all must suffer.
Like when the Etesian winds send storms from Thrace,
Sweeping over the darkened sea and whirlpools to land,
From the great depths of the ocean its ooze and sand
Crashes on the shore in wave after wave.

(Ant. 1)

I see sorrow on sorrow descending
On the family of Labacidus, from ancient times some god
Laid a curse on the family, and his stick
Beats each generation with endless sorrows.
The light that shone on its last son

Has gone out, and the bloody axe of fate
Has cut down that fine tree that used to blossom.
Oh Oedipus, brought down by your reckless pride!

(Str. 2)

What mortal power can fight against you, oh Zeus?
Not sleep that overcomes everything else,
Nor the moons that never tire: time cannot touch you,
On your throne in the dazzling light
On the peak of Olympus,
You reign as the all-powerful perfect King.
Past, present and future,
All bow to your orders;
Anything that rises above the common herd
Is punished by fate, whether it's love or hate.

(Ant. 2)

[Enter **HAEMON**]

Hope is always present, tireless,
She brings some wealth, some light love,
But nobody knows how her gifts can change
So that he'll suddenly be in hell.
It was an inspired wise man who said,
"If evil looks like good to anyone,
Then fate is waiting for them,
And they won't escape her punishment for long."
Here comes Haemon, your youngest,
And he is in an angry mood;
Is he sad for his bride,
Or the marriage he's cheated of;

Is he mourning for you,
Sad Antigone?

CREON

We'll soon know, better than any prophet can tell us;
Learning that the law has condemned your bride,
You don't intend, son, to blame your father?
Don't you know that everything I do is done from
love?

HAEMON

Oh father, I am your servant, and I will take
Your wisdom as my guide.
So no marriage is more important to me
Than your loving rule.

CREON

Well said; this is how right-minded sons should
behave,
Always bowing to their father's orders.
All parents hope that they will raise
Sons who are obedient, keen to avenge
The wrongs done to their father, and count his friends
as theirs.
But the one who breeds ungrateful sons,
He truly breeds trouble for himself,
And makes his enemies laugh. Son, be warned,
And never let a woman fool with your mind.
The husband married to a nagging woman is in
trouble,

And her embraces will soon lose their warmth.
For what cuts to the quick quite as much
As a false friend? So spit her out and throw her out,
Tell her to go and find a husband in hell.
For as I've caught her in open rebellion,
The one malcontent amongst all my subjects,
I will not be a traitor to the State.
She must die. Let her, if she wants,
Appeal to Zeus, the god of family, for
If I allow rebellion inside my house
Surely that will lead to rebellion outside.
The one who rules his own household well
Will prove to be a good ruler of a city.
But he who ignores the law, or thinks
He can ignore his rulers, that
I will never allow. Whoever the State
Chooses to lead must be obeyed in everything,
Big or small, just or unjust alike.
I say a man like this would be great,
Either as a King or a subject; such a man
Would stand his ground in the storm of battle,
A loyal and true comrade; but anarchy –
What evils anarchy does!
She ruins States and destroys the home,
She spoils and defeats armies;
While discipline keeps the ranks in order.
So we must keep our authority
And not allow a woman's wishes to outrank the law.
It would be better if men would throw me out
Than to hear it said, he was beaten by a woman.

CHORUS

To me, unless old age has made me stupid,
Your words seem reasonable and wise.

HAEMON

Father, the gods give mortal men
Reason, the greatest gift heaven has.
It's not for me to say you're wrong, and
I wouldn't find fault with your wisdom if I could;
And yet other men can have wise thoughts too,
And, as your son, it's my duty to note
The acts, the words, the comments of the crowd.
The public are terrified of your anger,
And dare not say anything that might offend you,
But I have overheard their muttered complaints
And know how they mourn this girl, sentenced
To the worst sort of death for her noblest actions.
When her own brother, killed in battle, lay
Unburied, she did not let his corpse
Lie out for the dogs and carrion birds:
They ask why her name isn't praised as high as
possible.
These are the rumblings I hear.
Oh father, nothing is more important to me
Than your wellbeing, for what better thing
Can a child want than a great reputation for their
father,
Just as fathers want the same thing for their sons?
So, father, don't stick to a fixed path,
Thinking you're right and all others are wrong.
For the person who thinks that he is wise,
Thinking that he's the only one who speaks or thinks
the truth,

Such thoughts are empty when tested.
The wisest man will let himself be influenced
By the wisdom of others, and change his position in
time.
See how the trees by a flooding stream
Survive, if they bend with the force, every flower
untouched,
But by resisting the whole tree falls.
The sailor who keeps his mainsail tight
And will not loosen it when gales blow, is likely
To find his ship overturned.
So relent and give up your anger;
For, if one young in years might claim to have some
sense,
I'll say the best thing is to have
Perfect wisdom, but, if that's not given,
(And nature doesn't often give such riches)
The next best thing is to listen to good advice.

CHORUS

If you think his words are to the point, then listen to
him, King.

(To **HAEMON**)

You listen to your father as well; you have both
spoken well.

CREON

What, do you think at my age I should be taught,
Lectured in judgment by a beardless boy?

—

HAEMON

I am asking for justice, father, that's all.
Judge me on my merits, not my youth.

CREON

It's a strange merit this, to want to allow her to break
the law!

HAEMON

I wouldn't speak up for real criminals.

CREON

And isn't this girl a confirmed criminal?

HAEMON

The Theban people unanimously say, no.

CREON

What, shall the mob dictate my policies?

HAEMON

It's you, I think, who's talking like a child.

CREON

Am I to do what I think right or what others tell me?

HAEMON

A State that is only the will of one man is no State at all.

CREON

The State belongs to its ruler, that is the custom.

HAEMON

So you would be good as king over a desert.

CREON

I think this boy supports the woman's cause.

HAEMON

Only if you're a woman. I'm thinking of you.

CREON

You scoundrel, are you going to argue with your father?

HAEMON

Because I see that you're being deliberately stubborn, and wrong.

CREON

Am I wrong to insist on my rights?

HAEMON

Don't talk about rights; you are going against Heaven.

CREON

You have had your heart turned, you're a slave to a woman!

HAEMON

But you'll never find me a slave to dishonor.

CREON

What you said was all pleading for her.

HAEMON

And for you, me, and the gods of the underworld.

CREON

The girl will never live to be your bride.

HAEMON

So she'll die, but someone else will die with her.

CREON

Has it come to this, that you are threatening me?

HAEMON

How is it threatening to criticize bad judgment?

CREON

You're a vain fool to lecture your superiors; you shall regret it.

HAEMON

If you weren't my father I'd say you're wrong.

CREON

Don't be a lapdog, you woman's slave.

HAEMON

So when you speak nobody can answer?

CREON

This is beyond belief. By god, you will not scold
And mock and disobey me without punishment.
Take that horrid thing away so she can die
At once, in the sight of her bridegroom, at his side.

HAEMON

Don't think the girl will die in my sight,
Or by my side; you shall never again
See my face from now on. Go and hang out with
People who want a madman for their friend.

[Exit **HAEMON**]

CHORUS

Your son has gone, my lord, with angry haste.
The anger of youth when reprimanded is fierce.

CREON

Let him go and blow off steam like a devil;
He won't save these two sisters from death.

CHORUS

Surely, you don't mean to kill them both?

CREON

I stand corrected; only the one who touched
The body.

CHORUS

And how is he to die?

CREON

She'll be taken to some deserted place
Where no man goes, and in a rocky cave,
With just enough food to avoid the stain
That murder might bring on the State,
Buried alive. There she can call for help from
The King of Death, the one god she respects,
Or she can learn the lesson, too late,
That it's a waste of effort to worship the dead.

CHORUS

(Str.)

Love cannot be resisted,
All surrender at a glance from you,
Love who lies all night
On a maiden's cheek,
Love holds all the cards.
Shouldn't men give in to you?

(Ant).

All you rule over are mad,
And even the wisest heart
Will become stupid at once,
When touched by your poisoned dart.
You started this fight,
This feud of blood on blood,
With the eyes of a charming wife.
And the desire to win her heart.
As the one who is joined
With the gods, next to Justice,

You make men do what you want,
All-powerful Love.
Look, I myself am led away
From Justice, when I look at this bride.
This is a sight which drowns the eyes in tears,
Antigone, so young, so lovely,
Rushed away
Into the home of the dead.

ANTIGO

Friends, countrymen, I make my last goodbye;
My journey is over.
I take one last sweet, lingering, longing look
At the bright sun.
For Death who can put to sleep both young and old
Drags my young life away,
And calls me down to the underworld,
An unmarried wife.
No youths have sung the marriage song for me,
My bridal bed
Has not been covered by girls with meadow flowers;
It's Death I'm marrying.

CHORUS

But think, you are going
To the underworld with glory.
You haven't been cut by a sword
Or ravaged by disease.
You are going unsullied
To the dead below.

ANTIGONE

No, I've heard the sad tale told
Of the doomed child of Tantalus,
Chained up high on the rock slopes of Siphylus,
Clinging to it like wild ivy,
Soaked by the pelting rain and whirling snow,
Left there to waste away
While the tears fall on her cold breast forever –
That is my fate.

CHORUS

She was born from the gods,
And we are mortals.
To become as famous as the gods
Will pay you for all your pain.
Take this comfort to your grave,
That you suffer her fate in life, have her fame in
death.

ANTIGONE

Alas, alas! You are mocking me. Is it right
To insult me to my face like this while I'm still alive?
Stop it, I pray you in the name of our holy places,
You lordly rulers of a lordly race.
Oh spring of Dirce, wood covered plain,
Where the Theban chariots rush to victory,
Look at the cruel laws which have damned me,
And the friends who show no pity in my trouble!
Did anyone ever have a fate like this? Oh terrible
sentence,

To be entombed within a rocky prison,
Unknown to both the living and the dead.

CHORUS

(Str. 3)

You were proud and hasty;
You madly kicked out
At the altar of Justice.
You carry a father's guilt.

ANTIGONE

That is what hurts me most,
My unlucky father's sad disgrace,
The stain of blood, the inherited stain,
That sticks to all of the famous family of Labadacus.
A curse on the terrible marriage bed where
A mother lay with the son she'd carried,
Where I was conceived, a curse on the day,
And now I die, cursed and unmarried,
To meet them as a stranger there below;
And you, my brother, ill-served by marriage,
It was you, dead, who dealt me the fatal blow.

CHORUS

Religion has her obligations, it's true,
And respect should be paid when it's due.
But it is bad to disobey
The powers who hold authority through strength.
You have defied that authority,

A willful rebel, and so you must die.

ANTIGONE

Unmourned, unmarried, friendless, I leave here,
And will no longer see the sun;
There's not one friend left to share my bitter sorrow,
And heave just one sigh over my remains.

CREON

If whining and tears could do anything
To keep death away, I'm sure nobody would ever
stop.
Take her away, and having walled her up
In a rocky tomb, as I ordered,
Leave her alone, free to die or,
If she chooses, to live alone,
With the tomb as her home. Either way
We are guiltless with regard to her death,
But she will find no home on earth.

ANTIGONE

Oh grave, oh bridal chamber, oh prison house,
Cut from the rock, my eternal home,
From where I go to join the great army
Of kinsfolk, the long dead guests of Persephassa,
The last of all and the most miserable
I go, my destined lifespan cut short.
And yet I am hopeful that I'll find
A welcome from my father, a welcome, too
From you, my mother, and my dear brother.

———

These hands washed and dressed your body
In death, and poured offerings on your grave.
My Polyneices, I paid you due respect,
And this is my reward!
But the wise know that I was right.
For even if you had been some child of mine,
Or a husband lingering at death's door,
I would not have gone against the State in this way.
Why do I say I was right then? This is how
I see it. If it had been a dead husband
I could have married again, and had
Another child, to take the dead child's place.
But my mother and father are both dead,
And no other brother can be born for me.
So by the laws of conscience I was led
To honor you, dear brother, and was judged
By Creon to be guilty of a terrible crime.
And now he drags me like a criminal,
An unwed bride, cheated of marriage song
And marriage bed and the joys of motherhood,
Left by my friends to a living grave.
What law of Heaven have I disobeyed?
After this can I look to any god
For relief, call on any man for help?
Alas, my piety is judged blasphemy.
Well, if this is the justice heaven approves,
I shall be punished for my sins;
But if the sin is theirs, may they suffer
Nothing worse than the wrongs they do me.

CHORUS

That same headstrong will

Still drives the girl like a gale.

CREON

So, the guards who have let her stay here
Shall be well punished for their delay.

ANTIGONE

Alas! Hearing these words
Brings death very close.

CHORUS

I can say nothing to comfort you. What he says
Means nothing other than death.

ANTIGONE

My fatherland, divine city of Thebes,
You gods of Thebes from whom my family comes,
You mighty lords of Thebes, all look on me;
You see the last survivor of your royal house.
Martyred by men, overcome;
This is what my piety has got me.

[Exit **ANTIGONE**]

CHORUS

(Str. 1)

You are like that bright maiden.

———

Danae, in her brass tower,
Who had to exchange the sweet sunlight
For a cell, which became her bridal chamber.
And yet she came from royal stock,
My child, like yours,
And nursed the child
She conceived
From Zeus coming to her as a golden rain.
The ways of fate are strange, her power
Cannot be resisted by wealth, or arms, or towers;
And brassclad ships, that plough through the sea,
Cannot escape fate.

(Ant. 1)

So Dryas' child, the unwise Edonian King,
As punishment for contemptuous words
Brought Bacchus to a rocky dungeon,
To calm down the madness of his fevered brain.
His frenzy passed
And he learned
That it was madness to throw insults at a god.
Once he tried to put out the nymphs' fire,
And provoked the anger of the Muses.

(Str. 2)

By the iron rocks that guard the two seas,
On the lonely shore of the Bosphorus,
Where Salmydessus' plain stretched
Into the wild lands of Thrace,
There on his borders Mars saw
The revenge taken by a jealous step-mother,

The gore that trickled from a red needle,
And the sightless eyes of her two stepsons.

(Ant. 2)

[Enter **TEIRESIAS** and BOY]

Wasting away they mourned their horrid fate,
The cursed issue of their mother's womb.
But she could trace her heritage
To the great Erectheus;
The daughter of Boreas, she was raised
In the great caves of her father where the storms rage;
She sped as swift as horses over the fields,
A child of gods; but like you my child
She was defeated by fate
Which never grows old or dies.

TEIRESIAS

Prince of Thebes, we are one traveler in two,
As we only have eyes for one; we are here.
The blind man cannot move without a guide.

CREON

What news, old Teiresias?

TEIRESIAS

I will tell you,
And when you hear you must listen to the prophet.

———

CREON

I've never gone against your advice.

TEIRESIAS

And that way you've governed well.

CREON

I know it, and gladly admit my debt to you.

TEIRESIAS

Be warned that once again
You are on the razor's edge of danger.

CREON

What is this?
Your words fill me with dread.

TEIRESIAS

I shall tell you what my skills have discovered.
Sitting in my prophet's seat,
As usual, where I can hear
What all the birds are saying, I heard
A strange racket of twittering, hoots and screams;
So I knew that all the birds were tearing at each other
With bloody claws, for the whirr of wings
Could mean nothing else. Feeling perturbed
I straight away tried a fire sacrifice

On the blazing altars, but the god of Fire
Did not give flame, and from the thigh bones there
dripped
And sputtered in the ashes a foul ooze;
Gall bladders cracked and spurted, the fat
Melted and fell and left the thigh bones bare.
These were the signs I read, described by this lad –
As I guide others, so this boy guides me –
The frustrating signs of oracles gone quiet.
Oh King, your headstrong temper is harming the
State,
For all our shrines and altars have been polluted
By the vomit of dogs and crows,
The flesh of Oedipus' unburied son.
Because of this the angry gods reject
Our prayers and our burnt offerings;
No birds can sing a happy note
With their throats stuffed with human gore.
Think of this, my son. All men
Make mistakes, but the man who is mistaken
Should not hold onto his mistakes, he repents and
looks
For a cure, if he's not stupid or wasteful.
There's no fool, the saying goes, like an obstinate
fool.
Let death calm your vengeance. Do not
Try to punish the dead. What glory will you win
From beating a dead corpse? I mean you well;
You always liked my advice if it promised good
things.

CREON

Old men, you all fire your arrows at me
Like archers at a target; now you set
Your fortune teller on me. You're all peddlers
And I'm the goods you buy and sell.
Get lost, and make your profits elsewhere,
Buy Indian gold with Sardinian silver,
But you'll never buy this man's burial,
Not if the winged messengers of Zeus
Carried him up to his throne in their claws;
Not even my fear of such things
Would make me permit his burial, for I know
No human stain can touch the gods.
I also know this, Teiresias; when skill
And cunning disguise foul treachery
With fair words then it's heading for a nasty fall.

TEIRESIAS

Alas! Do any know and remember –

CREON

Is this the opening for some clichéd old saying?

TEIRESIAS

How much good advice is the best thing of all?

CREON

True, as stupidity is the worst thing.

TEIRESIAS

You are infected with that yourself.

CREON

I won't trade insults with you, fortune teller.

TEIRESIAS

Yet you say my prophecies are false.

CREON

Prophets are in it for the profits.

TEIRESIAS

And all kings love money.

CREON

Do you know whom you're attacking, me, your lord?

TEIRESIAS

Lord and savior of the State – thanks to me.

CREON

You're a skilled prophet, but you lean towards evil.

TEIRESIAS

Be careful or you'll make me tell
The secret I have hidden deep inside.

CREON

Speak on, but make sure you're not speaking for your
profit.

TEIRESIAS

That's what you think I have been doing up to now.

CREON

Make sure you don't insult my intelligence.

TEIRESIAS

Then you should know for sure, that the sun
Will not have risen and set many times before
You will have given your own child
To pay for the murder you have done, life for life;
For you have buried a living soul,
And sent a living person to the underworld,
And wronged the gods of that place by leaving
A corpse unwashed, unmourned, unburied.
You have no say in this, not even the gods
Of heaven do; you are assuming a power that's not
yours.
For this the avenging spirits of Heaven and Hell,
Who chase down sinners, are on your trail:
You shall suffer what you have made others suffer.
And now, think about whether I have been bribed

To say this. For in a little while
The sound of men and women wailing
Shall be heard in your empty halls;
And all your neighboring States will ally to avenge
Their mangled warriors who have found their grave
In the mouth of a wolf or dog, or a bird
That pollutes their city's air as it flies home.
These are the arrows which I, like an archer,
Provoked to anger, fire at your breast,
Well aimed, and you shall not escape their wounds.
Boy, lead me home, leave him to insult
Younger men, and learn to hold his tongue
With better manners than he shows at present.

[Exit **TEIRESIAS**]

CHORUS

My lord, the man has gone, predicting sorrow.
And believe me, since these grey hairs
Were jet black, I have never known
The prophet's warning to the State to be wrong.

CREON

I know that, and it worries me.
To surrender is terrible, but the obstinate soul
Who fights against fate is badly beaten.

CHORUS

Son of Menoeceus, listen to good advice.

CREON

What should I do? Advise me, I will listen.

CHORUS

Go, free the girl from her rocky prison,
And build a tomb for the unburied outlaw.

CREON

That's your advice? You want me to surrender?

CHORUS

Yes, King, at once. The vengeance of the gods
Soon catches up with the unrepentant.

CREON

Ah! What a wrench it is to give up
What I'd set my heart on; but it's pointless to fight
Fate.

CHORUS

Go, don't trust others; do it yourself.

CREON

I'm hurrying there now. Get moving,
Bodyguards! Get axes! Hurry
To that mountain! I'll come too,

For now I'm set on this.
It was I who imprisoned her, I who'll set her free.
I'm almost convinced it's best
Always to stick to the old laws.

[Exit **CREON**]

CHORUS

(Str. 1)

You who are worshipped with many names,
Child of Zeus the god of thunder,
Born a miracle from a Theban bride,
The guardian of fair Italy;
In the deep buried places
Of Persephone,
The haunt of revelers, men and women,
You can be seen, Dionysus.
Where the river Ismenus flows,
Where the Dragon's teeth were sown,
Where you daughters, the Bacchanals,
Dance around you,
That's your home;
Thebes, oh Bacchus, belongs to you.

(Ant. 1)

We see you on the two crested rock,
With bright flaming torches;
Where the Corsican maidens flock
To you by the springs of Castille.
By Nysa's ivy-clad castle,

———

By the shores with their happy vineyards,
There the hymn is sung to you,
And in the streets we Thebans shout,
All praise to you,
Hail, hail!

(Str. 2)

As you love this city most of all,
To you, and your lightning-struck mother,
We call out in our great need;
You see what an illness strikes our townsfolk.
We crave your help,
Whether you come down from Parnassus,
Or come flying over the roaring sea,
Save us, save us!

(Ant. 2)

Brightest of all the stars,
Real son of Zeus, the immortal King,
Leader of all the voices of the night,
Come, and bring your Bacchantes with you,
Your frenzied followers,
Who dance before you all night long, and shout,
We are your handmaids,
Hail, hail!

[Enter **MESSENGER**]

MESSENGER

Listen all who live in the lands

Of Cadmus and Amphion. No man's life
Can be said to be just good or bad,
For fate ebbs and flows and
Throws down and elevates high and low alike,
And no man can tell the future.
Take Creon; he, I thought, of all men
Was to be envied. He saved this land
Of Cadmus from our enemies, gained
A king's powers and ruled the State alone,
And he had a noble son to seal his happiness.
Now it is all gone and ruined, for a life
Without life's pleasures I call a living death.
You'll tell me he has plenty of money,
And all the trappings that go with being a king; but if
These give no pleasure, I rate all the rest
As a ghostly shadow, nor would I exchange
His wealth and power for one drop of joy.

CHORUS

What fresh sorrow do you bring to the royal house?

MESSENGER

They're both dead, and there are those alive who
deserve death.

CHORUS

Who is the killer, who's the victim? Speak.

MESSENGER

Haemon, and his blood was not shed by a stranger's hand.

CHORUS

What do you mean? By his father's or his own?

MESSENGER

His own, in protest at his father's crime.

CHORUS

Oh prophet, what you predicted has happened.

MESSENGER

That's the situation; now you must act.

CHORUS

Look! From the palace gates I see coming
Creon's unhappy wife, Eurydice.
Has she come by chance or does she know her son's fate?

[Enter **EURYDICE**]

EURYDICE

You men of Thebes, I overheard your talk.
As I was going out to make my prayers

To Pallas, and was drawing back the bolts
To throw open the door, on my ears
There crashed a wail that told of a tragedy for the
household;
Struck down by terror I fell and fainted
In my handmaid's arms. But repeat your tale
To one who is used to misery.

MESSENGER

Dear mistress, I was there and will tell
The absolute truth, omitting nothing.
Why should we disguise and flatter, to be shown
As liars afterwards? The truth is always best.
Well, in attendance on my master, your lord,
I crossed to the farthest edge of the plain, where
The corpse of Polynieces, chewed and mauled,
Was still lying. We offered up a prayer
To Pluto and the goddess of crossroads,
With humble hearts, to soften their anger.
Then we washed the mangled corpse with purifying
streams,
Put fresh-cut branches on it, lit a pyre,
And in his memory piled up a great
Earth mound. Then we went to the rocky cave,
The place the girl was to married with Death,
As quickly as we could, and were about to enter. But
a guard
Heard from that godless place a far off scream,
And ran back to tell our lord the news.
But as he got nearer the hollow moans
Of mourning reached the King.
He groaned and said these bitter words:

"Am I a prophet? Oh misery!
Is this the saddest road I ever took?
That's my son's voice. Hurry on,
Guards, as fast as you can to the tomb
Where rocks have been torn down to make a gap,
look in
And tell me if I am right to think that was
The voice of Haemon, or am I tricked by heaven?"
So at the orders or our distraught lord
We looked, and in the cavern's gloom
I saw the girl lying there strangled
With a linen noose around her neck;
Right next to her, holding her cold body,
Was her lover, mourning his dead bride
Who had married death, and cursing his father's
cruelty.
When the King saw him, with a terrible groan
He went towards him, crying, "Oh my son,
What have you done? What troubled you? What
mishap
Has made you mad? Oh come outside,
Come out, my son, your father begs you."
But the son glared at him with fierce eyes,
Spat on his face and then, without a word,
Drew his two handed sword and struck, but missed,
His father flew backwards. Then the boy,
Furious with himself, poor wretch, uncontrollably
Fell on his sword and drove it through his side,
Then still breathing he held the girl in his
Weak arms, her white cheek reddened
With his dying breaths. So there they lay,
Two corpses, together in death. His marriage
ceremony

Will be performed in the underworld;
It shows that of all the evils in the world,
Men's stupidity is the worst.

[Exit **EURYDICE**]

CHORUS

What do you make of this? The Queen has gone
Without saying a word, good or bad.

MESSENGER

I'm surprised too, but don't be afraid.
I'm sure she doesn't want to mourn her son's sad
death
In public, and wants to mourn her private loss
In privacy with her handmaidens.
Trust me, she is careful and won't do anything wrong.

CHORUS

I don't know – I think strained silence
Can be a worse sign than excessive grief.

MESSENGER

Well, let's go inside and find out
Whether the storm in her heart has hidden
Some evil plan. It may be that you're right;
Unnatural silence is not good.

CHORUS

——

Look! The King himself is here.
He is carrying evidence of his guilt;
I fear to lay charges against a king,
But everyone must admit
That his guilt is his and his alone.

CREON

Alas for the sin of twisted minds,
Fatally wounded with a mortal curse.
Look at us, killed and killers, all alike.
Alas for my dreadful ideas, born of sin.
Alas, my son,
Your life had hardly begun,
And now it's over.
It was my fault, only my fault, my son!

CHORUS

It seems you've seen the truth too late.

CREON

I have learnt through sadness. The punishment of god
is heavy,
My feet have trodden thorny rough paths,
My pride is humbled and my pleasure turned to pain;
Poor mortals, how we slave away for nothing.

[Enter **SECOND MESSENGER**]

SECOND MESSENGER

You have sorrows, my lord, and there are more to come.
There is one lying at your feet, and a worse one
Awaits you when you come home.

CREON

How can there be any more sadness for me?

SECOND MESSENGER

Your wife, the mother of your dead son here,
Lies struck down by a recent blow.

CREON

How deep the pit is!
Do you want me too, oh Death?
What does he say,
This sad messenger? Is it right
To kill a man a second time?
Is Death at work again,
Blow after blow, first the son and now the mother
dead?

CHORUS

Look for yourself. There she is for all to see.

CREON

Alas! I see another sorrow.

What's left to add to my pain?
A minute ago I held a lifeless son,
And now Death has taken another victim.
Unhappy mother, most unhappy son!

SECOND MESSENGER

Beside the altar she fell on a keen edged sword
And closed her eyes in darkness, but first
She mourned for Megareus who nobly died
Long ago, then she mourned her son; with her last breath
She cursed you, the slayer of her child.

CREON

I shudder with fear.
Oh for a sharp sword to kill
A wretch like me,
Who is as one with misery.

SECOND MESSENGER

It's true that you were accused by the dead Queen
Of being guilty of both deaths, hers and her son's.

CREON

In what way did she kill herself?

SECOND MESSENGER

Hearing the loud mourning over her son

She stabbed herself through the heart.

CREON

I am the guilty one. I did the deed,
I'm the murderer. Yes, I plead guilty.
Guards, take me away, away, away!
I have no worth, I'm less than nothing; don't wait!

CHORUS

It's true that if anything good comes from disaster
It's that the suffering calls for the swiftest cure.

CREON

Come, friend, I need you now,
Hurry!
Come, my best friend,
Finish me!
Come on!
Don't let me see another day!

CHORUS

This is for tomorrow; at the moment there are
pressing matters
Which those whom they concern must deal with.

CREON

I join in your prayer which echoes my wishes.

CHORUS

Oh don't pray, prayers are useless; from the fate
Of Death there is no hiding place.

CREON

Take me away, a worthless wretch who killed,
Not meaning to, you, my son, and your mother too.
I don't know which way to turn; every way
Just leads to wrong,
And on my head I can feel the heavy weight
Of crushing fate.

CHORUS

The thing that's needed most for happiness
Is a wise heart:
To cheat the gods in anything
Is full of danger.
Great words, full of pride,
Are struck down mightily by the gods.
Punishment for past sins
Brings wisdom to age in the end.

Made in the USA
Middletown, DE
14 September 2022